Twenty to Make

Tasty Trinkets

Polymer Clay Food Jewellery

Charlotte Stowell

Search Press

First published in Great Britain 2010

Search Press Limited
Wellwood, North Farm Road,
Tunbridge Wells, Kent TN2 3DR

Text copyright © Charlotte Stowell 2010

Photographs by Debbie Patterson at
Search Press Studios

Photographs and design copyright
© Search Press Ltd 2010

ISBN: 978-1-84448-555-0

Suppliers
If you have difficulty in obtaining any of the
materials and equipment mentioned in this book,
then please visit the Search Press website for
details of suppliers: www.searchpress.com

Printed in Malaysia

Contents

Introduction

Polymer clay is an easy and enjoyable material to work with. It can be set permanently hard by baking in an ordinary oven. It has a very tactile and almost edible-looking quality, so is the perfect way to create miniature food jewellery masterpieces. Polymer clay colours are irresistibly delicious and you will soon be hooked on trying out the endless different ways of combining them to make beautiful patterns. This is also a very tolerant medium to work with, which can be twisted, rolled, blended and stretched into a vast range of decorative shapes.

Polymer clay is available from most good art and craft shops and also from online stockists. Look out for packs with mixed colour selections, which give a good range of different colours to get you started. Metallic and glittery polymer clays are also worth investigating, particularly for jewellery and bead-making projects, as they give an extra sparkle to your work. Small pieces like the ones in this book do not use up a lot of material, so once you have invested in a few basic colours, a little goes a long way.

Jewellery findings can be sourced inexpensively at bead shops or online, so designing homemade polymer clay jewellery is an economical way to create something really special.

As with all small-scale work, these projects need patience and perseverance to achieve good results, but your modelling skills will develop and improve with practice once the basic techniques have been mastered. Try making a rough version of a project to familiarise yourself with the technique before doing your finished version.

Remember that the measurements given here are only a guide, and the projects themselves are only suggestions. You will probably want to try experimenting with your own original variations on these ideas.

Basic techniques and tools

Work surface

Always use a clean, smooth work surface. A cutting mat with a sheet of smooth paper over the top is ideal as you can easily change the paper if necessary. Otherwise, wipe the cutting mat regularly.

Hands and nails

Long fingernails will dig into the polymer clay and create unwanted marks, so it is best to keep them short. Wipe your hands frequently with wet wipes, as dark polymer clay colours can transfer on to paler ones. Be particularly careful with white polymer clay as it easily picks up specks of dust and other colours.

Tools

You do not necessarily need to buy special tools for polymer clay modelling. Good results can be achieved with household tools and other small items like cocktails sticks or wooden stirring sticks, which are ideal for neatening edges and making holes. Sandpaper, cheese graters, sieves and sponges are all useful for adding texture. Keep a small rolling pin for polymer clay which is not used for food. You will need a small craft knife or scalpel for cutting polymer clay. Polymer clay blades sold in craft shops are the perfect way to make straight lines and clean slices, but use these with caution as they are incredibly sharp! Round-nosed pliers are the best way to make wire loops. You will also need cutting pliers for trimming chain and jewellery findings. Flat-nosed pliers are used to open and close jump rings and press crimp ends.

Cutting shapes

Small confectionary cutters are ideal for making neat shapes from polymer clay. An apple corer or pen lids make useful circle cutters.

Some shapes (such as the gingerbread man) are easier to cut out using a paper template as a guide. Place the template on to rolled-out polymer clay, then carefully cut round it with a small craft knife. For symmetrical shapes, draw half the shape on to folded paper, then cut it out.

Conditioning clay and blending

Some polymer clay can be stiff when it is first opened. Knead it before you begin modelling, or try rolling it out with a rolling pin and folding it a few times to make it easier to work with. To make small quantities of paler shades and pastel colours, knead bright polymer clay colours with white. For blending large quantities, roll the colours together with a large rolling pin or use a pasta machine (my machine has only ever been used once to make pasta). Keep rolling and folding until you have an even blend.

6

Baking polymer clay

Polymer clay needs to be baked at a very low oven temperature to set it permanently hard. Put your polymer clay work on to a baking tray then follow the manufacturer's instructions for precise temperatures.

Making holes in beads

Carefully push a needle through polymer clay shapes to make holes. If the beads are going to be threaded, the holes needs to be wide enough for the cord to pass through without getting stuck, widen the holes with a cocktail stick if necessary. Do this before baking, and be careful not to distort the shape.

Paint and varnish

Where paint effects are required, use ordinary acrylic paints. A layer of varnish gives a glossy finishing touch to polymer clay and will also help to keep any small pieces in place. Push an eye pin or headpin into the hole (made for the jewellery finding) so the varnish can be brushed on without touching your piece of work. Leave to dry with the end of the pin pushed into a piece of unbaked polymer clay.

Jewellery findings

Mini screw eyes are ideal for polymer clay as they have a fine screw thread, which can be securely fixed into small holes once your pieces are hardened. If you can't find these, snip the end of an eye pin and glue this into the hole instead.

Clockwise from bottom left: cutting mat, metal leaf, cheese grater, sieve, sandpaper, natural sponge, polymer clay, rolling pin, polymer clay blade, wooden stirrers, pen lid, cocktail sticks, needle, craft knife, wet wipes, jewellery findings, small confectionery cutters.

Hot Stuff Chilli Charm

Materials:

Polymer clay – red
  and lime green

Headpins or eye pins

Varnish

Mini screw eyes

Jump rings

Chain

Hook clip for the end

Tools:

Cocktail stick or
  modelling tool

Needle

Brush for varnish

Cutting pliers

Flat-nosed pliers

Instructions:

1 Roll some red polymer clay into a 1cm (³/₈in) diameter ball. Roll some green polymer clay into a ball 8mm (⁵/₁₆in) diameter for the stalk.

2 Roll a red ball between your fingers until it stretches to 3cm (1¼in) long, then roll one end a bit more to make it thinner.

3 Roll the green ball into a stalk shape, stretching out one end to make it thinner.

4 Use a cocktail stick or modelling tool to mark small lines around the base of the stalk. Push the stalk on to the top of the chilli.

5 Smooth out the chilli with your fingers, curl the end, then bend the stalk over. Make four more chillies. Make holes in the bases of the stalks with a needle.

6 Bake to set hard, then cool.

7 Push headpins (or eye pins) into the holes so the chillies can be varnished without touching them. Leave to dry, then remove the headpins.

8 Push a screw eye into the hole in each chilli, then attach a jump ring so they can be fixed on to a chain with a hook clip on the end.

Pretty Peppers

This charm has yellow, green and orange peppers which will look great brightening a bag or purse.

Cup Cake Brooch

Materials:

Polymer clay – glittery purple, pink and green

PVA glue

Silver leaf – or use kitchen foil or foil sweet wrappers

Strong glue – for gluing the pin on to the back

Brooch pin

Tools:

Rolling pin

3cm (1¼in) circle cutter or circular lid

Knife or polymer clay blade

Cocktail stick or modelling tool

Small soft paintbrush

Instructions:

1 Roll a 3cm (1¼in) ball of glittery purple polymer clay to 3mm (⅛in) thick. Cut out a 3cm (1¼in) diameter circle, then slightly elongate it into an oval shape.

2 Cut a rectangle 3cm x 2cm (1¼in x ¾in) from the remaining rolled polymer clay. Cut a triangle slice from each side to make the cake case shape. Use a modelling tool, cocktail stick or knife to make a pattern of vertical lines.

3 Roll a 3cm (1¼in) ball of glittery purple polymer clay to 5mm (¼in) thick. Cut four strips 4cm (1½in) long x 5mm (¼in) wide.

4 Twist the strips into spirals. Place them on to the rolled oval shape.

5 Curl the ends down over the edges of the oval. Pull the top strip into a point.

6 Roll a 2cm (¾in) ball of pink polymer clay to 1mm (¹⁄₁₆in) thick. Cut a strip with an uneven edge 5cm x 1cm (2 x ⅜in) and roll it up to make a flower. Make a second flower.

7 Roll a tiny piece of green clay to 1mm (¹⁄₁₆in) thick. Cut out a small leaf.

8 Press the flowers and leaf on to the cake. Bake the cake and the case separately to set hard, then cool.

9 Brush a thin layer of PVA glue on to the cake case. Carefully lay the metal leaf on top, working it into the lines with a dry brush.

10 Use strong glue to stick the case in position on the bottom half of the oval, and to fix the brooch pin to the back.

Cup Cake Creations

Make minature cakes using the same method, then glue them on to blank ring findings. These make great gifts for people who like to have sweet things at their fingertips!

Bakery Delights Bracelet

Materials:

Polymer clay – pale browns
  in several shades, red
  and white
Brown acrylic paint
Varnish
Mini screw eyes
Jump rings
Bracelet chain with a clasp

Tools:

Rolling pin
Craft knife
Scourer or old
  toothbrush
Needle
Brushes for paint
  and varnish

Flat-nosed pliers
Cutting pliers
Pen lid for
  cutting circles

Instructions:

All the different bread shapes are
made from a 1.5cm (⁵⁄₈in) diameter
ball of pale brown polymer clay.

1 For the iced bun, slightly flatten
the ball between your fingers. Roll
a thin 1.5cm (⁵⁄₈in) diameter circle of white polymer clay
for the icing, shaping the edges if necessary to make
them wavy, then press it on to the flattened ball. Roll a
tiny ball of red clay for the cherry.

2 For the bread, squeeze a ball of polymer clay into an
oval shape, then cut diagonal lines across the top. For a
baguette make a longer, thinner shape.

3 For the croissant, roll a ball of pale yellow/brown
polymer clay to 2mm (¹⁄₈in) thick, then cut it into a 4cm
(1½in) long triangle shape with a craft knife. Roll up the
triangle and curl the sides in.

4 To make the palmier, roll a ball of pale brown polymer clay into a thin sausage 3mm (1/8in) in diameter then curl it into a spiral from both sides.

5 To make the plait, pinch three thin sausages of polymer clay together, then plait them and form into a loaf shape.

6 For the Chelsea bun, roll a 1cm (3/8in) diameter ball of pale brown polymer clay into a 5cm (2in) long sausage shape. Twist it round into a spiral, starting at the bottom and working upwards to the top of the bun.

7 Make a Chelsea bun as above. Thinly roll a small ball of white clay for the icing, shaping the edges if necessary to make them wavy. Press the icing on to the bun and add a red cherry in the middle.

8 Add texture to all the cakes with a scourer or an old toothbrush. Make a tiny hole in the edge of each shape for the screw eyes. Bake to set hard, then cool. Add some brown acrylic paint with a dry brush or small sponge, then varnish. Push mini screw eyes into the holes, then attach a jump ring to each piece and fix them on to a chain bracelet.

Doughnut Delight

To make a ring-shaped doughnut, push a pencil into the top of an iced bun shape so the icing is pushed down inside the middle. Make a selection of different colours with thin strands of icing across the top, and others with tiny icing blobs.

Cute Candy Necklace

Materials:

Polymer clay – white, lilac,
  orange, pink, brown
  and green

Cotton cord

Crimps, jump rings and clasp

Tools:

Rolling pin

Craft knife

Cocktail stick

Needle

Note

All the colours for
the dolly mixtures
were blended
with white to give
a more candy-
coloured feel to
the necklace.

Instructions:

For the round sweets:

1 Roll a 2cm (¾in) diameter ball of white polymer clay into a sausage shape with
your fingers. It should be 6cm (2³⁄₈in) long and 8mm (⁵⁄₁₆in) in diameter.

2 Shape a 3cm (1¼in) diameter ball of lilac polymer clay then elongate with your
fingers into a thick sausage shape. Flatten it with a rolling pin to 6mm (¼in) thick,
then wrap it around the thin white sausage.

3 Join the ends of the lilac polymer clay together around the sausage, then roll
gently, pulling outwards until the edges are smooth and the roll is 1cm (³⁄₈in) in
diameter.

14

4 Cut slices 1cm (³⁄₈in) thick from the end with a craft knife, then make holes through the middle of each piece with a needle. Repeat to make pink, brown, orange and green sweets.

For the square sweets:

5 Roll a white ball and an orange ball from polymer clay, making them roughly the size of a walnut, 3cm (1¼in) in diameter.

6 Slightly flatten the two balls with your fingers, then press them together and roll with a rolling pin to 1cm (³⁄₈in) thick.

7 Cut 1cm (³⁄₈in) squares with a craft knife to make little cube shapes. Make a hole through the middle of each piece with a needle.

For all beads:

8 Bake to set hard then cool. Thread the beads on to cotton cord. You will need around fifty mixed beads for a necklace. Fix crimps to the ends of the cord, then add jump rings and a clasp.

Sweets for my Sweet

The Liquorice Allsorts necklace is a striking and fun alternative. To make sweets with more stripes (like the black and white ones), simply add four or five flattened balls in layers, roll them together and cut into slices.

Jam Tart Earrings

Materials:

Polymer clay – pale
 brown and red

Varnish

Mini screw eyes

Jump rings

Earring wires

Tools:

Rolling pin

2.5cm (1in) diameter
 lid for cutting
 circles

Button

Cocktail stick or
 modelling tool

Scourer or old
 toothbrush

1.5cm ($^5/_8$in) diameter
 lid or cutter

Flat-nosed pliers

Cutting pliers

Craft knife

Brush for varnish

Needle

2, 3

Instructions:

1 Roll out some pale brown polymer
clay to 5mm (¼in) thick. Use a 2.5cm (1in)
diameter lid to cut two identical circles.

2 Smooth the edges of a circle with your fingers, then push a button
(or use the flat end of a smaller lid) to made a depression 1.5cm ($^5/_8$in)
diameter in the centre.

3 Use a modelling tool to cut small lines around the edge of the circle with the button (or
lid) still in place to help to keep a circular shape. Remove the button when you have gone
all the way round. Repeat with the second circle to make another pastry case.

4 Roll red polymer clay to 2mm ($^1/_{16}$in) thick. Make a texture on the surface with a sponge
scourer or toothbrush. Cut out two 1.5cm ($^5/_8$in) diameter circles using a small cutter or a lid.

5 Press the red circles into the pastry case shapes. Cut tiny hearts from the pastry colour
using a craft knife and add to the middle of each tart.

6 Make two smaller tarts in the same way. Add tiny cut-out circles to the middles.

7 Carefully make holes with a needle in the top of the big tarts and at the top and bottom of the small ones.

8 Bake to set hard then cool. Varnish the jam and leave to dry.

9 Push mini screw eyes in to the tops and bottoms of the small tarts and the tops of the big ones. Add jump rings and attach them to earring wires.

Tasty Tarts

These earrings look good enough to eat with orange and purple centres suggesting apricot and plum jam. Find a jam colour to match your favourite outfit!

Christmas Charm

Materials:

Polymer clay – brown, white, red, green and yellow

White paint

Strong glue

Varnish

Mini screw eyes

Jump rings

Chain

Lobster clasp

Ribbon

Tools:

Sandpaper

Rolling pin

Flower mini cutter or craft knife

Cocktail stick or modelling tool

Craft knife

Needle

Small sponge

Cutting pliers

Flat-nosed pliers

Brush for varnish

Instructions:

Christmas pudding

1 Roll a 2.5cm (1in) ball of brown polymer clay. Roll it on some coarse sandpaper to give it a texture.

2 Flatten a small piece of white polymer clay to 1mm (¹⁄₃₂in) thick with a rolling pin. Cut the topping using a flower-shaped mini cutter or cut freehand with a craft knife.

3 Press the white topping on to the pudding. Add holly leaves cut from 1mm (¹⁄₃₂in) thick green polymer clay. Use a cocktail stick or modelling tool to mark the central lines of the holly leaves. Roll tiny red berries for a finishing touch.

Yule log

4 Flatten out 3cm (1¼in) diameter brown and yellow polymer clay balls to 3mm (¹⁄₈in) thick with a rolling pin. Cut both colours into 6 x 4cm (2³⁄₈ x 1½in) rectangles.

5 Place the two pieces together with the yellow on top.

6 Roll the two colours together into a spiral. Keep rolling and stretching until you have a smooth cylinder 1.5cm (⁵⁄₈in) in diameter. Cut off a 2.5cm (1in) length and add lines with a cocktail stick or modelling tool.

7 Make holly as for the Christmas pudding and bake it. Make a small hole in the top of the log with a needle and bake separately from the holly. Using a small sponge, apply a dusting of white paint over the log. Glue the holly leaves and berries on top.

Candy cane

8 Roll red and white polymer clay sausage shapes around 6cm (2³/₈in) long and 5mm (¼in) in diameter.

9 Twist the two pieces together. Keep rolling and twisting until the stripes look the right distance apart, then cut off a 5cm (2in) length and shape into a candy cane.

For all three pieces

10 Make a small hole in the top of each shape with a needle. Bake to set hard, then cool. Varnish. Fix mini screw eyes and jump rings. Attach the charms to chains with a clasp on the end.

11 Tie a small ribbon around the candy cane.

Candy Canes

Have a charming Christmas with this festive trinket! You can make three candy canes in different colours as an alternative.

Gingerbread Charm

Materials:

Polymer clay – brown, white, red, green, yellow and lilac

Varnish

Mini screw eyes

Jump rings

Chain

Lobster clasp

Tools:

Scissors

Rolling pin

Craft knife and cutting mat

Garlic press

Needle

Brush for varnish

Cutting pliers

Flat-nosed pliers

Instructions:

1 Photocopy the template shapes and then cut them out.

2 Flatten some brown polymer clay with a rolling pin to 3cm (1¼in).

3 Carefully cut around the templates with a craft knife.

4 Remove the templates and smooth down the edges of the house, star and gingerbread man with your fingers.

5 Use the garlic press to make very thin strands of brightly coloured polymer clay, and also make tiny rolled balls. Decorate the shapes with the strands and balls.

6 Make a small hole in the top of each shape with a needle.

7 Bake all the shapes to set hard, then cool. Varnish.

8 Fix mini screw eyes into the holes then add jump rings on a chain with a lobster clasp.

Star of my Heart

Add white 'icing' to gingerbread shapes made with mini cutters. Glue on tiny silver beads.

Swiss Roll Earrings

Materials:

Polymer clay – white and
 dark brown

Mini screw eyes

Jump rings

Earring wires

Tools:

Rolling pin

Craft knife or polymer
 clay blade and
 cutting mat

Sandpaper

Needle

Flat-nosed pliers

3

Instructions:

1 Flatten out a 3cm (1¼in) ball of white polymer clay to 5mm (¼in) with a rolling pin. Cut a rectangle 4 x 5.5cm (1½ x 2¼in).

2 Flatten out a ball of dark brown polymer clay to 5mm (¼in) in the same way. Cut a rectangle 4cm x 6cm (1½ x 2³⁄₈in) so it is slightly longer than the white one.

3 Place the white rectangle on top of the brown one, then roll them together.

4 Slice off the end using a craft knife or polymer clay blade, to make it smooth. Cut two 1cm (³⁄₈in) slices from the roll.

5 Reshape the rolls into circles with your fingers if they have become squashed. Add a cake texture with sandpaper and make a small hole in the top of each roll with a needle.

6 Bake to set hard, then cool.

7 Fix mini screw eyes into the holes. Attach with jump rings to earring wires.

Let Them Wear Cake!

To make these fun jam roll earrings, use exactly the same method,
replacing the white and brown with red and pale yellow.

Burger Bracelet

Materials:

Polymer clay – light brown, dark brown, green, red, yellow and dark pink

Brown paint

Varnish

Mini screw eyes

Jump rings

Chain

Clasp

Tools:

Craft knife and cutting mat or flower confectionery cutter

Sandpaper

Cocktail stick or modelling tool

Needle

Rolling pin

Garlic press

Brush

Flat-nosed pliers

Cutting pliers

Instructions:

Burgers

1 Roll three balls of light brown polymer clay. Cut them all in half across the middle so the top half is slightly bigger then the bottom half. Smooth the edges into a bun shape.

2 Flatten three 1cm (³/₈in) diameter balls of dark brown clay into burger shapes. Press them on to sandpaper to create texture and flatten them round the edge.

3 Cut three 1 x 1cm ((³/₈ x ³/₈in) squares from very thinly rolled yellow polymer clay for the cheese. Flatten three small balls of red polymer clay for the tomato sauce.

4 Cut lettuce leaves from thinly rolled green polymer clay using a flower-shaped mini cutter or a craft knife. Shape the edges with a cocktail stick.

5 Stack the burgers, lettuce, tomato sauce and cheese on to the bottom halves of the buns then add the top pieces. Make holes in the tops with a needle.

Hot dogs

6 Roll two 1.5cm (⁵/₈in) balls of light brown polymer clay into long bun shapes. Cut each one along the top to make a split.

7 Roll dark pink sausages and place them into the buns. Add thin strands of yellow polymer clay along the top in a wavy pattern to make mustard. I used a garlic press but you could make these by hand. Make holes in the ends of the hot dog buns with a needle.

For both:

8 Bake to set hard then cool. Lightly brush the buns with brown paint. Leave them to dry, then varnish them. Fix mini screw eyes into the holes. Attach jump rings around a chain with a clasp to finish the bracelet.

Fries to Go!

Shape the carton from a strip of red and make a hole at the bottom for a headpin. Bake the fries separately so they can be glued into position inside the carton. Make a loop at the top of the headpin and attach a jump ring and earring wire.

Pizza Necklace

Materials:

Polymer clay – pale brown, yellow, red, green and black

Varnish

Mini screw eye

Cotton cord

Crimps

Jump rings

Clasp

Tools:

Rolling pin

3cm (1¼in) circle cutter or lid

Cocktail stick or modelling tool

Needle

Brush for varnish

Flat-nosed pliers

Instructions:

1 Roll out some pale brown polymer clay with a rolling pin to 5mm (¼in) thick. Cut a 3cm (1¼in) diameter circle using a cutter or circular lid.

2 Roll a sausage of pale brown polymer clay 5mm (¼in) in diameter x 10cm (4in) long. Carefully wrap it around the edge of the circle.

3 Roll some red polymer clay to 2mm (⅛in) thick. Cut out a 3cm (1¼in) diameter circle then press around the edges to make a slightly irregular shape.

4 Place the red piece on the pizza. Sprinkle tiny pieces of sliced yellow polymer clay on to the pizza for the cheese. Add some green pieces on top.

5 Roll minature balls of black polymer clay 3mm (⅛in) diameter for the olives. Push a cocktail stick through the middles to make holes, then add to the pizza.

6 Push a needle into the side of the pizza.

7 Bake to set hard then cool. Varnish.

8 Fix a mini screw eye into the hole, then thread a length of cotton cord through it. Attach crimps to the ends of the cord and add a jump ring on to one end and a clasp to the other.

Charmingly Cheesy

Make the pizza base in the same way as for the necklace, with a yellow circle added to the inside instead of red, then cut it into six equal slices. Sprinkle on different coloured toppings.

Fondant Fancy Earrings

Materials:

Polymer clay – pink and white or yellow and dark brown

Varnish

Mini screw eyes

Jump rings

Earring wires

Tools:

Cocktail stick or modelling tool

Craft knife

Garlic press

Needle

Brush for varnish

Flat-nosed pliers

2 —

Instructions:

1 Roll two 1.5cm (⁵⁄₈in) diameter balls of pink or yellow polymer clay. Press them into cubes.

2 Roll an 8mm (⁵⁄₁₆in) ball of pink or yellow polymer clay, then cut it in half. Press one piece on to the top of each cube.

3 Press out thin strands of white or dark brown polymer clay using a garlic press. Use them to make a zigzag swirl of icing on the top of each cake.

4 Make a hole in the top of each cake with a needle.

5 Bake the cakes to set hard, then cool them and varnish them.

6 Fix mini screw eyes into the holes. Attach them with jump rings on to earring wires.

Chocolate Orange Heaven

Press 1.5cm (⁵/₈in) balls of polymer clay into flattened square shapes with rounded corners as cake beads for this necklace. Add swirls and stripes for the patterns.

Chocolate Bar Earrings

Materials:

Polymer clay – dark brown

Varnish

Mini screw eyes

Jump rings

Earring wires

Tools:

Rolling pin

Craft knife and
  cutting mat

Large needle

Two wooden stirring
  sticks (or lolly sticks)

Brush for varnish

Flat-nosed pliers

5

Instructions:

1 Roll out some dark brown polymer
clay to 8mm (⁵/₁₆in). Cut out two 2 x 3cm
(¾ x 1¼in) rectangles.

2 Holding both ends of a large needle, mark out
the squares of chocolate by lightly pressing on to
the polymer clay rectangles. Reshape using wooden
stirring sticks if necessary to keep an even shape.

3 Check the squares are evenly spaced, then press down again
with the needle to make the lines deeper.

4 Carefully flatten around the edge of the top of the chocolate blocks
with a wooden stirring stick so the squares in the centre look slightly raised.

5 Make a hole in the top of each chocolate block with a needle. Reshape
into rectangles using the stirring sticks before baking.

6 Bake to set hard, then cool. Varnish and leave to dry.

7 Fix screw eyes into both the chocolate blocks, then attach on to a jump
rings and earring wires.

Chocolate Chic

For the necklace alternative, use PVA glue to stick on a piece of gold metal leaf and a strip of silver foil at the top to look like wrapping. Carefully use a dry brush on the gold leaf so the block pattern is still visible underneath. Make this irresistible treasure for a chocoholic friend!

Stylish Sushi Earrings

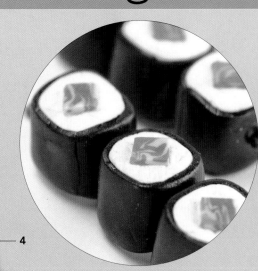

Materials:

Polymer clay – white, black and two shades of pink

Varnish

Two headpins

Earring wires

Jump rings

Tools:

Rolling pin

Small chain – for making texture

Craft knife or polymer clay blade and cutting mat

Thick needle

Brush for varnish

Flat-nosed pliers

Round-nosed pliers

— 4

Instructions:

1 Roll six 1.5cm (⁵/₈in) diameter balls of white polymer clay into short cylinder shapes for the middles of the sushi.

2 Roll out a 3cm (1¼in) diameter ball of black polymer clay with a rolling pin to 1mm (¹/₃₂in) thick. Cut it into 3 x 1.2cm (1¼ x ½in) strips and wrap these around the sushi.

3 Use a small piece of chain to make a rice-like texture in the white polymer clay.

4 Roll 1cm (³/₈in) balls of light pink and dark pink polymer clay into sausages 4cm (1½in) long. Twist them together and flatten several times with a rolling pin to 1mm (¹/₃₂in) so the colours are streaky. Cut out six 5 x 5mm (¹/₈ x ¹/₈in) squares. Place one on top of each piece of sushi.

5 Use a needle to carefully make a hole right through each piece. Twist the needle round to ensure the hole will be wide enough for a headpin to pass easily through the middle.

6 Bake to set hard and cool. Varnish and leave to dry.

7 Thread three sushi beads on to each headpin. Bend the tops into loops with round-nosed pliers, then attach to earring wires with jump rings.

Oriental Charm

Use the same method to make a sushi charm. These sushi are wrapped in dark green polymer clay and have more elaborate decorations on top.

Slices of Cake Earrings

Materials:

Polymer clay – pale
  yellow, dark brown,
  white, red and green

Mini screw eyes

Jump rings

Earring wires

Varnish

Tools:

Cocktail stick or
  modelling tool

Rolling pin

Craft knife or polymer
  clay blade and
  cutting mat

Needle

Brush for varnish

Flat-nosed pliers

5

2

Instructions:

1 Roll out a 3cm (1¼in) ball of pale
yellow polymer clay to 5mm (¼in) thick.
Cut it into a rectangle 3 x 5cm (1¼ x 2in)
then cut in half to make two 3 x 2.5cm
(1¼ x 1in) rectangles.

2 Roll out a 2cm (¾in) ball of brown polymer clay
to 3mm (⅛in) thick. Cut a rectangle 3 x 2.5cm (1¼ x
1in) then place it between the two yellow rectangles
to make a sandwich.

3 Lightly roll the sandwich with a rolling pin without reducing the thickness too
much. Cut out two small triangle shapes to make slices of cake.

4 Roll a 2cm (¾in) diameter ball of brown polymer clay to 2mm (⅛in) thick, cut
it into a long rectangle 2 x 6cm (¾ x 2⅜in).

5 Place one of the cake slices on to the rolled brown polymer clay. Cut around
the base of the triangle, then wrap the brown 'icing' over the back and top of
the cake slice, cutting it to fit. Do the same with the second piece.

6 Cut two thin strips of brown polymer clay 2mm x 1.5cm ($\frac{1}{8}$ x $\frac{5}{8}$in). Twist round to decorate the tops of the cakes. Form tiny strawberries from red polymer clay with green hulls and add texture with needle. Place blobs of white polymer clay 'cream' on the cake slices with a strawberry on top of each. Make a hole in the top of each strawberry with a needle.

7 Bake to set hard and cool. Varnish.

8 Fix mini screw eyes into the holes, then add jump rings and attach the cakes onto earring wires.

Cake Lover's Bracelet

Try different colour combinations to make cake slices for a sweet-looking charm bracelet.

Rainbow Lolly Brooch

Materials:

Polymer clay – red, orange, yellow, green, blue and purple

Varnish

White stick from a cotton bud or a painted cocktail stick

Strong glue

Brooch pin

Tools:

Rolling pin

Craft knife or polymer clay blade and cutting mat

Cocktail stick or modelling tool

Brush for varnish

Instructions:

1 Roll out 1.5cm ($^5/_8$in) diameter balls of red, orange, yellow, green, blue and purple polymer clay into 8cm ($3^1/_8$in) long strands.

2 Twist all the strands together. Roll and stretch them into one long, smooth strand, 5mm (¼in) in diameter.

3 Cut off a piece 20cm (8in) long. Coil it into a circle.

4 Make a small hole with a cocktail stick next to the end of the coil.

5 Bake to set hard, then cool. Varnish the lolly and leave it to dry.

6 Glue a white cotton bud stick (or painted cocktail stick) into the hole. Glue the finished lolly on to a brooch pin.

Lollipop, Lollipop

Roll thinner, shorter strands of brightly coloured polymer clay to make smaller matching lollies for a charm.

Battenberg Cake Earrings

Materials:

Polymer clay – pale
  yellow, pale pink
  and dark yellow
Mini screw eyes
Jump rings
Earring wires

Tools:

Rolling pin
Craft knife or polymer
  clay blade and
  cutting mat
Needle
Flat-nosed pliers

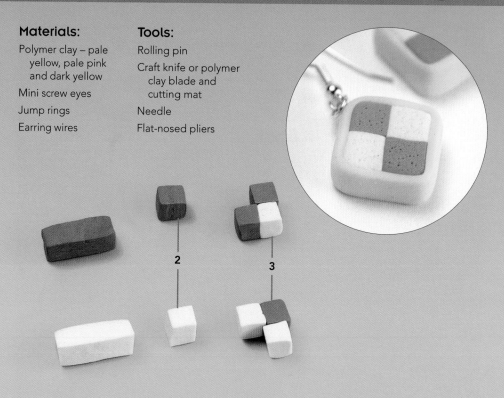

Instructions:

1 Roll a 3mm (⅛in) diameter ball of pale yellow polymer clay to 8mm (⁵⁄₁₆in) thick
with a rolling pin. Repeat with a pink ball of the same size. Trim the edges straight
with a craft knife or polymer clay blade.

2 Cut 6mm (¼in) wide strips from both colours of rolled polymer clay. Cut four
squares, 6 x 6mm (¼ x ¼in), from each strip so you have eight squares altogether.

3 Arrange two pink squares and two yellow squares together with matching
colours diagonally opposite each other. Do this again for the second piece.

4 Press very gently over the squares with a rolling pin so the squares are
pushed together.

5 Roll a 3mm (⅛in) ball of darker yellow polymer clay with a rolling pin into a
long rectangle 2mm (¹⁄₁₆in) thick. Cut two 8mm x 8cm (⁵⁄₁₆ x 3⅛in) strips and wrap
them around the squares, trimming the end if necessary. Use your fingers to
smooth where the two ends join.

6 Make a hole in the corner of each slice of cake with a needle.

7 Bake to set hard, then cool.

8 Fix mini screw eyes into the holes. Attach jump rings and earring wires.

Chocolate Checkerboard Necklace

People either love or hate Battenberg cake with its marzipan coating, but who wouldn't love these earrings, full of nostalgia for childhood tea times? Use the same method for making a chocolate checkerboard cake design with more squares.

Ice Cream Cone

Materials:

Polymer clay – pale brown, white and dark brown

Mini screw eye

Two jump rings

Cotton cord

Two crimps

Glue

Clasp

Tools:

Rolling pin

3cm (1¼in) circle cutter or lid

Craft knife and cutting mat

Cocktail stick or modelling tool

Pencil

Needle

Flat-nosed pliers

2

Instructions:

1 Flatten a 2cm (¾in) diameter ball of pale brown polymer clay to 2mm (¹⁄₁₆in) with a rolling pin. Cut out a 3cm (1¼in) circle, then cut off the top third.

2 Use a craft knife to make a criss-cross pattern on the larger part of the circle. Roll it around the end of a pencil to make a cone shape.

3 Bake to set hard, then cool.

4 Roll a 3cm (1¼in) ball of white polymer clay into a sausage 6cm (2³⁄₈in) long, then roll it flat with a rolling pin to 5mm (¼in) thick. Cut a strip 5mm (¼in) wide and twist it on top of the cone in a spiral.

5 Cut a thin chocolate stick from brown polymer clay rolled to 2mm (¹⁄₁₆in) thick. Make it look flaky by pressing a craft knife along the sides.

6 Make a hole in the top of the ice cream with a needle for the mini screw eye, and another larger hole where the chocolate stick can later be glued.

7 Bake the finished ice cream cone and chocolate stick separately to set hard, and cool.

8 Glue the chocolate stick in place and fix a screw eye into the ice cream. Fix a jump ring on to the screw eye and thread a length of cotton cord through it. Attach a crimp and a jump ring to each end of the cord, and attach a clasp.

Two-tone Ices

Use different colours to suggest two flavours in each cone for this icy charm.

Strawberry Earrings

Materials:

Polymer clay – red, green, white and yellow

Varnish

Mini screw eyes

Jump rings

Chain

Earring wires

Tools:

Cocktail stick

Rolling pin

Pen lid, 1.3cm (½in) in diameter

Craft knife and cutting mat

Sandpaper

Pencil

Needle

Brush for varnish

Flat-nosed pliers

Cutting pliers

3

4

5

Instructions:

1 Roll six 1cm (³/₈in) balls of red polymer clay.

2 Pinch the ends with your fingers to make strawberry shapes.

3 Use a cocktail stick or needle to make a dotty pattern.

4 Roll green polymer clay to 2mm (¹/₈in) thick with a rolling pin. Cut six circles using a pen lid 1.3cm (½in) in diameter. Cut the circles into star shapes using a craft knife and push them on to the tops of the strawberries to make hulls.

5 Roll a 2cm (¾in) ball of white polymer clay to 2mm (¹/₈in) thick with a rolling pin. Press out two white circles using the pen lid and cut into flower shapes with a craft knife. Press a tiny yellow ball into the centre of each flower.

6 Make holes in the tops of the strawberries and the flower petals with a needle.

7 Bake to set hard then cool. Varnish and leave to dry.

8 Fix screw eyes into the strawberries and jump rings into the flowers. Attach them to two short pieces of chain in a cluster with jump rings. Fix earring wires at the end.

Citrus Burst Earrings

Make clusters of oranges, lemons and limes. The leaves are made from glittery green polymer clay.

Harvest Time Brooch

Materials:

Polymer clay – pale brown, red, dark green, bright green, yellow, pale green and orange

Varnish

Strong glue

Brooch pin

Tools:

Rolling pin

Tea light holder or cutter, to cut a 4cm (1½in) circle

Garlic press

Craft knife and cutting mat

Cocktail stick

Felt pen lid

Pencil

Brush for varnish

Instructions:

1 Roll a 3cm (1¼in) ball of pale brown polymer clay to 3mm (⅛in) thick. Cut a 4cm (1½in) diameter circle using a tea light holder or cutter. This is the base of the basket.

2 Push a ball of the same colour polymer clay into a garlic press. Squeeze and add more polymer clay until you can cut off strands 12cm (4¾in) long.

3 Coil four layers of strands on to the circle to build up the sides of the basket. Add six 1cm (⅜in) strands inside the basket. Bake to set hard and cool.

4 For the tomatoes, roll 1cm (⅜in) balls of red polymer clay. Roll out some very thin dark green polymer clay, cut out tiny circles using a pen lid, and cut them into star shapes using a craft knife. Push these on top of the tomatoes.

5 For the lettuce, flatten twelve 1cm (⅜in) diameter balls of bright green polymer clay with your fingers. Shape the edges so they are uneven then roll them around each other.

44

6 For the corn, roll a 1.5cm (⁵/₈in) ball of yellow polymer clay into a corn cob shape. Use a craft knife to mark a pattern, then wrap the corn in three long leaves cut from thinly rolled, pale green polymer clay.

7 For the carrots, roll 1cm (³/₈in) balls of orange polymer clay into carrot shapes. Use a craft knife to make lines around each carrot and make holes in the tops with a pencil. Cut leaves from rolled bright green polymer clay and push them into the hole.

8 Arrange the vegetables in the hardened basket and press them gently together. Bake to set hard and cool. Squeeze some strong clear glue under the vegetables to make sure they are securely fixed to the basket, then varnish and leave to dry. Glue a brooch pin to the back.

Pumpkin Earrings

Use 2.5cm (1in) diameter balls of orange polymer clay for pumpkin earrings. Press a short brown stalk into a hole in the top and attach a mini screw eye to the stalk.

Melon Slice Earrings

Materials:

Polymer clay – red/pink mix, white, glittery green and black

Varnish

Mini screw eyes

Jump rings

Earring wires

Tools:

Rolling pin

Craft knife or polymer clay blade and cutting mat

Brush for varnish

Needle

Flat-nosed pliers

— 2 —

Instructions:

1 Roll a 2cm (¾in) diameter ball of blended red/pink polymer clay. Roll a 2.5cm (1in) ball of white polymer clay and use a rolling pin to flatten it to a 2mm (⅛in) thick circle.

2 Wrap the rolled white circle around the red ball. Cut away any folds so it is the same thickness all the way round. Roll it smooth.

3 Roll a 3cm (1¼in) diameter ball of glittery green polymer clay. Flatten it with a rolling pin into a circle shape 2mm (⅛in) thick.

4 Wrap the rolled glittery green circle around the white ball in the same way as before, cutting away any folds and rolling it smooth.

5 Use a polymer clay blade or an extended craft knife to carefully slice the ball in half, then cut off two wedge-shaped sections. Reshape each wedge if necessary.

6 Press tiny black polymer clay 'seeds' on both sides of the wedges. Make a small hole in the top of each piece with a needle.

7 Bake to set hard, then cool. Varnish and leave to dry.

8 Fix mini screw eyes into each piece of melon. Add jump rings and earring wires.

Oranges and Lemons

To make these alternative fruity earrings, use the same method as for the melon and use a craft knife to mark the pattern on the segments.

Publisher's Note
If you would like more books on polymer
clay modelling, try the following:
Twenty to Make: Polymer Clay Bears
by Birdie Heywood, Search Press 2010

You are invited to visit the author's website:
www.charlottestowell.com

Acknowledgements
All FIMO soft polymer modelling clay and
other FIMO modelling products featured
in this book were supplied courtesy of
STAEDTLER (UK) Ltd
www.staedtler.co.uk

Also thanks to Beadz Bazaar for supplying
some of the jewellery findings:
www.beadz.co.uk